✪ WEAPONS OF WAR
MILITARY
VEHICLES
1980 TO TODAY

A⁺

Smart Apple Media

© 2015 Smart Apple Media, an imprint of Black Rabbit Books
P.O. Box 3263, Mankato, Minnesota, 56002
www.blackrabbitbooks.com

Published by arrangement with Amber Books

Contributing authors: Chris Chant, Steve Crawford, Martin J. Dougherty,
Ian Hogg, Robert Jackson, Chris McNab, Michael Sharpe, Philip Trewhitt

Special thanks to series consultant Dr. Steve Potts

Photo credits: Art-Tech/Aerospace, Cody Images, Corbis, U.S. Department of Defense

Illustrations: © Art-Tech/Aerospace

Library of Congress Cataloging-in-Publication Data

Trewhitt, Philip.
Military vehicles : 1980 to today / Philip Trewhitt & Chris McNab.
pages cm. — (Weapons of war)
Includes index.
ISBN 978-1-62588-044-4
1. Armored vehicles, Military — History. 2. Tanks (Military science) — History.
I. McNab, Chris, 1970- II. Title.
UG446.5.T743 2015
623.74'7--dc23
                                    2013034773

Printed in the United States at Corporate Graphics,
North Mankato, Minnesota
PO1649
2-2014

9 8 7 6 5 4 3 2 1

CONTENTS

Introduction

Armored Warfare

Armored warfare will be at the center of modern military strategy for the forseeable future.

While main battle tanks (MBTs) often capture the attention of the media and enthusiasts, their role on the modern battlefield is actually a rather minor one. For of all the factors that contribute to combat success, vehicle logistics always ranks among the most important. Without the ability to transport soldiers and materiels from the industrial base to the actual frontline, an army will be unable to wage war.

During the last 60 years, military strategists and tacticians have alternately praised and maligned the armored fighting vehicle. With the advent of nuclear weapons, efficient anti-armor missiles and mines, it seemed at one time that the day of the tank had passed. However, armored vehicle technology has advanced as well, and the role of the tank has been redefined to the battlefield of the twenty-first century and beyond. Through decades of warfare, the key attributes of firepower, speed, and armor protection have guided the development and deployment of the tank. The armored vehicle itself has been redesigned, fitted with futuristic equipment and armament and integrated into the general battle plans of nations across the globe.

OFFENSIVE PROWESS

New technology has revolutionized armored vehicle design. Most modern tanks are armed with a smoothbore cannon. Rifled guns are inherently more accurate, but smoothbore guns can fire fin-stabilized rounds at a higher pressure, which means greater velocity and greater penetration. Protection for crew members has been improved by the use of tough composite armor made from layered laminates of plastics, ceramics, steel and rare — but very dense — metals like depleted uranium.

As a result, tank weights have increased dramatically, but developments in engine technology have more than compensated for the increase. Multi-fuel diesels or gas turbine engines now deliver up to 1500 hp (1,118 kW), which is enough to drive a 59-ton (60-tonne) tank at more than 43.5 mph (70 km/h) on roads. Sophisticated suspension systems make

4

EE-9 CASCAVEL: see page 37

them almost as fast across rugged terrain. Similar improvements have enhanced the capabilities of other armored fighting vehicles, which are tougher, more mobile, and more effectively armed than they have ever been before.

The effectiveness of the MBT has been demonstrated in combat and shows continuing improvement in multiple aspects of design and tactical capacity. Heavier, more versatile platforms mount specialized turrets housing larger caliber guns capable of firing APFSDS (armor-piercing fin-stabilized discarding sabot) ammunition and, in some cases, anti-tank missiles. Stabilization systems allow main battle tanks to fire on the move with great accuracy, while laser rangefinding and infrared night-vision equipment facilitate target acquisition and compensate for atmospheric conditions in a variety of climates and weather conditions.

Battlefield management systems allow the tracking of multiple targets simultaneously, assisting in the identification of both friendly and hostile vehicles, while advanced communications equipment coordinate operations on a grand scale. Increasingly powerful engines, such as the conventional diesel or gas turbine types, provide speed, reliability, and ease of maintenance.

Defensive modernization includes the introduction of composite, modular, and

AMX-10: see page 28

LUCHS: see page 53

CENTAURO: see page 33

explosive reactive armor, isolated storage space for ammunition with blast doors to protect crew members, and components designed to direct an explosion outwards in case the tank's hull or turret is penetrated by enemy attack.

Warning sensors designed to alert the tank crew to an imminent threat when the vehicle is "locked on" by enemy laser equipment coordinate with appropriate countermeasures to minimize the likelihood of a direct hit. Smoke grenade launchers are standard on the modern MBT, while machine guns remain a necessity for protection against low-flying aircraft or attacking infantry. NBC (nuclear, biological, and chemical) defensive systems allow

10

ROOIKAT: see page 51

armored vehicles to operate in such adverse conditions.

Modern low-intensity combat, such as that seen in Afghanistan and Iraq since 2001, has nevertheless constituted a persistent paradox for the armored fighting vehicle. The confines of urban warfare often limit the capabilities of the tank during close-in fighting, while rudimentary improvised explosive devices (IEDs) and land mines remain hazards to even the latest in technologies. In response, defensive packages specifically designed for low intensity and urban combat have been introduced.

ARMOR IN IRAQ

The M1A1 and M1A2 Abrams main battle tanks made up the bulk of the US heavy

WEAPONS OF WAR

M998 HUMMER: see page 46

armor during the Iraq War, each an improved version of the original M1 Abrams. While a number of the early M1s were upgraded to the M1A1 in the field during the Gulf War of 1991, the M1A2 went into production in 1992. A number of existing tanks were also upgraded to the M1A2. Mounting the same main gun as the M1A1, the reliable 120mm M256 adaptation of the Rheinmetall smoothbore (originally utilized in the German Leopard 2 main battle tank), the M1A2 contained extensive upgrades, with an independent thermal viewer and weapons control for the tank commander along with enhanced navigation and radio equipment. The M1A2 SEP (System Enhancement Package) includes FBCB2 (Force XXI Battlefield Command Brigade and Below) communications capabilities, improvements to the engine cooling system, digital maps, and upgraded armor that incorporates depleted uranium.

AFGHANISTAN INTERVENTION

Since 2001, the US, United Kingdom and subsequently NATO forces have been involved in the effort to end Taliban rule, quell the subsequent insurgency, and destroy the al-Qaeda terror network in Afghanistan. While heavy armor has been utilized to project firepower, particularly during heavy fighting for control of cities and urban areas, mountainous terrain has limited its mobility,

M2 BRADLEY: see page 44

often confining the main battle tank to roads and areas clear of mines and IEDs.

Light armored vehicles such as the M2/M3 Bradley fighting vehicle, the Humvee and the Land Rover Wolf utility vehicle have proved their value as patrol and rapid response vehicles. The Land Rover Wolf has been a mainstay of the British forces in both Iraq and Afghanistan. The Wolf traces its lineage to the Land Rover company's fearsome light truck and transport vehicles of the World War II period.

The US Army's Stryker series of infantry fighting vehicles are also playing a vital role in Afghanistan. Already well known for its deployment to Iraq, the first Stryker unit arrived in Afghanistan in 2009. Developed from earlier Canadian and Swiss designs, the Stryker entered service with the US Army in 2002 to complement the older M2/M3 Bradleys. Conceived as a method of rapidly introducing combat troops to the battlefield, the Stryker carries up to nine soldiers and is armed with a 12.7mm machine gun or 40mm grenade launcher mounted in the Protector M151 remote weapons station, which may be operated from the relative safety of the vehicle's interior.

TAM: see page 56

WEAPONS OF WAR

BMP-2: see page 30

ADVANCE WEAPON TECHNOLOGY

While the British Challenger 2 and the German Leopard 2 main battle tanks remain preeminent among modern European main battle tank designs, France, Poland, Italy, and others have entered their own MBTs into production in recent years. Since its deployment during Operation *Iraqi Freedom* and to Bosnia and Kosovo, the Challenger 2 has continued to undergo refinement. According to the British government, numbers of MBTs and their role are changing within the military, including the consolidation of several armored squadrons and the allocation of one armored regiment to focus primarily on reconnaissance. The Challenger Lethality Improvement Program is currently in progress and includes the possible replacement of the 120mm (4.7in) L30 rifled gun with the 120mm (4.7in) Rheinmetall L55 smoothbore, which is common to the German Leopard 2. Enhanced NBC (nuclear, biological, and chemical) defenses are also being evaluated.

Meanwhile, the Challenger 2E emerged in response to the necessity of fighting and maintaining combat efficiency in extreme climates. Competing directly with the Leopard 2 and other MBTs for export to other countries, the Challenger 2E was produced from approximately 2002 to 2005. Extensive trials took place in the deserts of the Middle East, and the Challenger 2E remains equipped with the 120mm L30 rifled gun. However, its combat skill was augmented by a battlefield communications and management system that allows for the tracking of multiple targets simultaneously and provides enhanced acquisition and ranging. Thermal sights were improved for both the commander and gunner, while the commander may also operate the turret independently. It was upgraded with the 1500 hp (1,125 kW) Europack MTU 883 diesel.

LEAP OF THE LEOPARD

The most recent version of the Leopard 2, the 2A6, was the first of the German tanks to mount the longer 120mm L55 smoothbore gun. An auxiliary engine has been added in the 2A6 along with air conditioning and enhanced protection against landmines, with some of these tanks designated 2A6M. The German Army began upgrading more than 200 of its frontline tanks to the 2A6 configuration in 2000, and the first deliveries of production 2A6s occurred the following year. Another variant of the 2A6, the 2E, offers greater armor protection and was developed in a cooperative effort by German and Spanish engineers. Still another version, the Leopard PSO, includes combat survivability systems designed for urban warfare.

WARRIOR: see page 58

Throughout its service life, the Leopard 2 has remained a popular export tank. The armies of Denmark, the Netherlands, Greece, Canada, Portugal, Spain, and Switzerland are among those fielding the MBT today. It has been deployed in the Balkans and to Afghanistan, engaging in notable firefights with Taliban and guerrilla forces.

LECLERC AND ARIETE

The first production main battle tank designed and manufactured in France in more than 30 years is the Leclerc. Although the early development of a new tank had begun in the 1970s, the Leclerc did not enter production until 1990. France and the United Arab Emirates worked in partnership on the tank and share the expense of development and production.

EE-T1 OSORIO: see page 38

Replacing the aged AMX-30 in French armored formations and in the armed forces of the United Arab Emirates, the Leclerc was not intended for major export or a lengthy production run, and fewer than 1000 were built by the time production ceased in 2008. France now has over 400 Leclercs in service and the United Arab Emirates Army over 380, delivered in 2004. The Leclerc has been deployed to Kosovo and with peacekeeping forces in Lebanon; however, it has yet to see substantial combat.

With the Leclerc, French engineers initially rejected the British Chobham armor and developed their own protection package by the 1990s. Emphasis has been on armor protection with composite steel and titanium sandwiching non-explosive and non-energetic reactive armor (NERA). Active countermeasures include a top speed of 44 mph (71 km/h) for rapid relocation and evasion, along with the Galix defense

CHALLENGER 2: see page 36

WEAPONS OF WAR

ABRAMS M1: see page 43

system that utilizes infrared screening rounds, smoke grenades, and anti-personnel weapons against attacking infantry.

The Italian firms Iveco Fiat and OTO Melara combined efforts to develop the C1 Ariete main battle tank, which has been deployed with the nation's armed forces since the mid-1990s. The Ariete is armed with a 120mm OTO Melara smoothbore cannon and protected by a classified composite armor thought to be comparable to that of contemporary main battle tanks. The tank is equipped with modern target acquisition and sighting equipment, allowing effective operations day or night. Active defenses include smoke grenade dischargers and the RALM laser warning receiver, which sounds an alarm when the tank is "painted" by hostile target acquisition systems.

INFANTRY FIGHTING VEHICLES

The German Marder, which entered service in 1971 and is currently being retired in favour of the Puma, was the first infantry fighting vehicle designed and developed by a NATO country for the specific purpose of transporting troops to a combat area and providing direct fire support for their operations. It was followed by the British Warrior and the American M2/M3 Bradley. The infantry fighting vehicle has remained significant in supporting infantry operations and providing protection to troops on the ground, while it has also performed well in a reconnaissance role. Given the need for scout, reconnaissance, and patrol types, several European nations have developed their own light armored vehicles. These have been deployed with NATO and United Nations peacekeeping forces in the Middle East and the Balkans and proved popular on the thriving export market.

A new generation of self-propelled artillery has also emerged during the last decade as many NATO countries replace their aging US-made M109 weapons systems. The German Panzerhaubitze 2000 entered production in 1998 and mounts a 155mm L52 gun developed by Rheinmetall, and more than 400 are in use with the armed forces of Germany, Italy, the Netherlands, and Greece. A European contemporary is the British AS-90, in service since 1993 and mounting the 155mm L31 cannon.

NEW TACTICS

Along with the ever-improving technology, battlefield tactics have also been refined. Recent battlefield experience has confirmed the tank's ability to create and to exploit a break in enemy lines, rapidly advance across favorable terrain, and hold territory in cooperation with armored infantry. These highly-mobile ground troops go into battle aboard armored personnel carriers

MERKAVA: see page 47

or infantry fighting vehicles designed not only to provide transportation but also to add direct fire support with a variety of powerful weapons from light machine guns to anti-tank missiles, chain guns, and high-velocity cannon. The MBT, its accompanying armored fighting vehicles, self-propelled artillery, and other types are destined to play active roles in ground warfare well into the future. As technology is continually refined, these vehicles will serve as primary weapons systems in any armed conflict of great magnitude.

Akatsiya 2S3M2

The 2S3 Akatsiya, or Acacia, was designated the SO-152 by its Soviet manufacturers. The 2S3 was developed in the late 1960s to counter the American 155 mm M109 self-propelled howitzer and it entered service with the Red Army in 1971. Since that time, it has continued to outfit armored formations of the forces of former Soviet republics while it has been exported to at least a dozen countries. By the end of the 1980s, Soviet armored and motorized rifle divisions each contained up to three battalions of the 2S3, totalling as many as 54 weapons. The chassis is the modified Objekt 123 tracked vehicle, which also powers the 2K11 Krug air-defense missile system. It has been upgraded a number of times since, most notably in 2000, when the M2 model was equipped with an automatic fire control system and a satellite navigational system and armed with a new 155 mm M-385 howitzer.

SPECIFICATIONS

COUNTRY OF ORIGIN: Soviet Union/Russia
CREW: 4
WEIGHT: 34,540 pounds (15,700 kg)
DIMENSIONS: length 25 feet 6 inches (7.75 m); width 10 feet (3.25 m); height 8 feet 7 inches (2.62 m)
RANGE: 310 miles (500 km)
ARMAMENT: 155 mm M-385 howitzer; 1 x 7.62 mm PKT machine gun
POWERPLANT: 1 x 520-hpV-59 V-12 multi-fuel diesel
PERFORMANCE: road speed 37 mph (60 km/h)

Al-Khalid Main Battle Tank

The Al-Khalid MBT was developed with assistance from China. Main armament is a 125 mm smoothbore gun that can fire conventional projectiles or missiles. These are of a Russian design produced in China under license and can engage both ground targets and low-flying helicopters. The gun is fitted with an autoloader, which helps keep the crew requirement down to three personnel (commander, driver, and gunner). This in turn contributes to a design that is somewhat smaller and lighter than Western main battle tanks. Armor is composite, with an overlay or reactive armor blocks. NBC protection is fitted, as is a laser-warning system. An auxiliary power system allows the electronic systems and sensors to operate while the engine is not running. The Al-Khalid can be fitted with a dozer blade, or a snorkel for river crossings. A Chinese-built version is available for export.

SPECIFICATIONS

COUNTRY OF ORIGIN: China/Pakistan
CREW: 3
WEIGHT: 103,617 pounds (47,000 kg)
DIMENSIONS: length 33 feet (10.07 m); width 11 feet 6 inches (3.5 m); height 7 feet 11 inches (2.435 m)
RANGE: 992 miles (450 km)
ARMOR: composite armor, RHA, ERA
ARMAMENT: 1 x 125mm smoothbore gun, plus 1 x 12.7mm external AA MG and 1 x 7.7mm coaxial MG
POWERPLANT: 1200 hp (890 kW) KMDB 6TD-2 6-cylinder diesel
PERFORMANCE: speed 45 mph (72 km/h)

AMX-10

In the 1950s, the French Army issued a requirement for a replacement for the standard Panhard EBR armored car with a more powerful armament. The first prototype of the AMX-10 was completed in 1971 and the vehicle entered service in 1979. The two main drawbacks were cost (being more expensive to build than some main battle tanks) and level of sophistication, particularly important for a conscript army. The suspension could be adjusted for different types of terrain and the fire-control system was the most sophisticated installed in any vehicle of its class, with a laser rangefinder, computer and low-light TV system, and complete amphibious capability. The internal layout is conventional, with driver at the front, a three-man turret, and engine and transmission at the rear.

SPECIFICATIONS

COUNTRY OF ORIGIN: France
CREW: 4
WEIGHT: 33,880 pounds (15,400 kg)
DIMENSIONS: length 30 feet (9.15 m); width 9 feet 8 inches (2.95 m); height 8 feet 10 inches (2.68m)
RANGE: 500 miles (800 km)
ARMOR: 0.31–1.25 inches (8–32 mm)
ARMAMENT: 1 x 105 mm gun; one 7.62 mm machine gun
POWERPLANT: 1 x Baudouin Model 6F 11 SRX eight-cylinder diesel developing 260 hp (194 kW)
PERFORMANCE: maximum road speed 53 mph (85 km/h); fording amphibious; vertical obstacle 2 feet 3 inches (0.70 m); trench 3 feet 9 inches (1.15 m)

Arjun Mk 1

The Arjun is India's first indigenous main battle tank design. The Indian Army's Combat Vehicle Research and Development Establishment encountered numerous problems with the project, resulting in significant delays, which held up the in-service date until 1994. One of the main problems was the lack of an indigenous powerplant, which forced the Indians to use a German MTU diesel. The Arjun's main armament is a locally designed stabilized 120 mm rifled gun capable of firing a variety of ammunition types, such as high explosive, high explosive antitank and high explosive squash head. The tank has an advanced fire-control system integrated with a combined day/night thermal imaging gunner's assembly with built-in laser rangefinder. In addition, there is a full weather sensor package.

SPECIFICATIONS

COUNTRY OF ORIGIN: India
CREW: 4
WEIGHT: 127,600 pounds (58,000 kg)
DIMENSIONS: 32 feet 2 inches (length 9.8 m); width 10 feet 5 inches (3.17 m); height 8 feet (2.44 m)
RANGE: 250 miles (400 km)
ARMOR: classified
ARMAMENT: 1 x 120 mm gun; one 7.62 mm machine gun
POWERPLANT: 1 x MTU MB 838 Ka 501 water-cooled diesel developing 1400 hp (1044 kW)
PERFORMANCE: maximum road speed 45 mph (72 km/h); fording 3 feet 3 inches (1 m); vertical gradient 3 feet 7 inches (1.1 m); trench 9 feet 10 inches (3 m)

BMP-2

First seen in public in 1982, the BMP-2 was designed to supplement rather than replace the BMP-1, having an almost identical chassis. Its low silhouette and long sloping front is useful in that it presents a small target. This is vital because its armor is extremely poor. One remarkable feature is that the rear doors are hollow and serve as fuel tanks, with obvious dangers for the troops inside. There are few concessions to comfort — the crew compartment being very crowded and uncomfortable — although the troops can fire their weapons from within. The two-man turret has the commander on the right and the gunner on the left, the 30 mm cannon having a powered elevation for use against helicopters and slow-flying aircraft. The BMP-2 saw action in Afghanistan.

SPECIFICATIONS

COUNTRY OF ORIGIN: Soviet Union/Russia
CREW: 3 + 7
WEIGHT: 32,120 pounds (14,600 kg)
DIMENSIONS: length 22 feet (6.71 m); width 10 feet 4 inches (3.15 m); height 6 feet 7 inches (2 m)
RANGE: 375 miles (600 km)
ARMOR: classified
ARMAMENT: 1 x 30 mm cannon; one At-5 anti-tank missile launcher; one 7.62 mm coaxial machine gun
POWERPLANT: 1 x Model UTD-20 6-cylinder diesel engine developing 300 hp (223 kW)
PERFORMANCE: maximum road speed 40.6 mph (65 km/h); fording amphibious; vertical obstacle 2 feet 4 inches (0.7 m); trench 8 feet 2 inches (2.4 m)

BMP-3

The BMP-3 entered service in 1990. Classified as an Infantry Combat Vehicle, its extensive armament almost places it in the category of small tank. Its turret boasts a 100 mm gun, which can fire either conventional shells or AT-10 laser-guided ATGWs. Alongside this weapon is a 30 mm cannon and the turret also bears a 7.62 mm PKT coaxial machine gun. Another machine gun is set in the forward hull. Despite the increase in stored ammunition and the consequent extra space this takes up, the BMP-3 takes only one less soldier than the BMP-1 (seven instead of eight), though it is more than three feet longer.

SPECIFICATIONS

COUNTRY OF ORIGIN: Soviet Union/Russia
CREW: 3 + 7
WEIGHT: 41,200 pounds (18,700 kg)
DIMENSIONS: length 23 feet 5 inches (7.14 m); width 10 feet 6 inches (3.23 m); height 8 feet 8 inches (2.65 m)
RANGE: 370 miles (600 km)
ARMOR: steel (details classified)
ARMAMENT: 1 x 100 mm gun; 1 x 30 mm cannon; 2 x 7.62 mm PKT MG
POWERPLANT: 1 x UTD-29M 10-cylinder diesel, developing 500 hp (373 kW)
PERFORMANCE: maximum speed 43 mph (70 km/h); fording amphibious; gradient 60 percent; vertical obstacle 2 feet 8 inches (0.8 m); trench 8 feet 2 inches (2.5 m)

BTR-90

The BTR-90, an Infantry Combat Vehicle, was first used in 1994. It is similar to the BTR-80 in general appearance and can carry 10 fully armed soldiers within its armored and amphibious hull. What makes it distinctive is its armament. All its weaponry is mounted in a single turret located towards the front of the vehicle and it consists of one 30 mm 2A42 automatic cannon, a coaxial 7.62 mm PKT machine gun, an automatic grenade launcher, and four AT-5 Spandrel anti-tank missiles. The spectrum of weaponry allows it to engage the enemy infantry, armor, and aircraft equally.

SPECIFICATIONS

COUNTRY OF ORIGIN: Soviet Union/Russia
CREW: 3 + 10
WEIGHT: 37,500 pounds (17,000 kg)
DIMENSIONS: length 25 feet 1 inches (7.64 m); width 10 feet 6 inches (3.2 m); height 9 feet 9 inches (2.97 m)
RANGE: 370 miles (600 km)
ARMOR: not disclosed
ARMAMENT: 1 x 30 mm 2A42 automatic cannon; 1 x coaxial 7.62 mm PKT MG; 1 x automatic grenade launcher; 4 x AT-5 Spandrel ATGWs
POWERPLANT: 1 x V8 diesel, developing 210 hp (15 7kW)
PERFORMANCE: maximum road speed 50 mph (80 km/h); fording amphibious

Centauro

The Centauro is officially described as a tank hunter. However, its armor is light compared to an MBT and a Centauro crew would rarely tackle an enemy tank in open battle. On top of an IVECO chassis is an OTOBREDA turret armed with a 105 mm gun. This weapon is capable of penetrating over 27.56 inches (700 mm) of armor at a range of around 6550 feet (2000 m) using armor-piercing fin-stabilized discarding-sabot (APFSDS) rounds. Gun handling and targeting are assisted by laser range-finding and a fully computerized fire control system like that used on the Ariete MBT. As an 8 x 8 vehicle, the Centauro has good off-road mobility assisted by hydropneumatic suspension and central tire-pressure regulation.

SPECIFICATIONS

COUNTRY OF ORIGIN: Italy
CREW: 4
WEIGHT: 55,100 pounds (25,000 kg)
DIMENSIONS: length (with gun) 28 feet 1 inches (8.55 m); width 9 feet 8 inches (2.95 m); height 2.73 m (8 feet 11 inches)
RANGE: 500 miles (800 km)
ARMOR: steel (details classified)
ARMAMENT: 1 x 105 mm gun; 1 x 7.62mm coaxial MG; 1 x 7.62 mm AA MG; 2 x 4 smoke grenade launchers
POWERPLANT: 1 x Iveco MTCA 6-cylinder turbo diesel, developing 520 hp (388 kW)
PERFORMANCE: maximum speed 67 mph (108 km/h); fording 4 feet 11 inches (1.5 m); gradient 60 percent; vertical obstacle 1 feet 10 inches (0.55 m); trench 3 feet 11 inches (1.2 m)

Challenger 1

The Challenger 1 was introduced in 1982 as a replacement for the Chieftain. It reflected British thinking on tank design, being heavily armed and armored. It was slower than contemporary Warsaw Pact vehicles, but made up for it with its composite Chobham armor, which was virtually impenetrable to enemy rounds, and the greater accuracy of its armament. In any case, NATO thinking regarding the war in central Europe with the forces of the Soviet Union and her allies, always placed the emphasis on defense and holding enemy forces until reinforcements arrived. Its armor and nimbleness, despite its lack of speed, allow for good survivability. As tanks become more complicated, this is important as the tanks are often easier to replace than their crews.

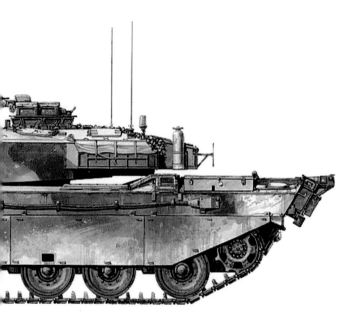

SPECIFICATIONS

COUNTRY OF ORIGIN: United Kingdom
CREW: 4
WEIGHT: 136,400 pounds (62,000 kg)
DIMENSIONS: length (gun forward) 35 feet 4 inches (11.56 m); width 10 feet 8 inches (3.52 m); height 7 feet 5 inches (2.5 m)
RANGE: 250 miles (400 km)
ARMOR: classified
ARMAMENT: 1 x 120 mm gun; 2 x 7.62 mm machine guns; 2 x smoke dischargers
POWERPLANT: 1 x liquid-cooled diesel engine developing 1200 hp (895 kW)
PERFORMANCE: maximum road speed 35 mph (55 km/h); fording 3 feet 3 inches (1 m); vertical obstacle 2 feet 11 inches (0.9 m); trench 9 feet 2 inches (2.8 m)

Challenger 2

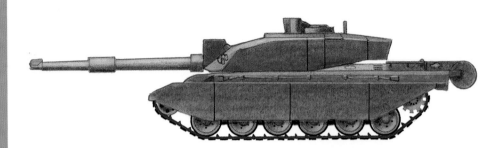

The Challenger 2 is one of the current main battle tanks of the British Army. The hull is similar to that of the Challenger 1, as is the powerpack, but the turret has been redesigned to fit updated armament and the tank is in many ways a completely new tank. The first production versions appeared in mid-1994, boasting a carbon dioxide laser rangefinder, and thermal-imaging and fully computerized fire-control systems, giving a high first-round hit probability. In addition, turret traverse is all electric and the gun is fully stabilized. It also has the capacity to be fitted with the Battlefield Information Control System in future years, to give even greater combat capability. A dozer can be fitted to the front of the hull. Nearly 400 were ordered by the British Army, with 18 being exported to Oman.

SPECIFICATIONS

COUNTRY OF ORIGIN: United Kingdom
CREW: 4
WEIGHT: 137,500 pounds (62,500 kg)
DIMENSIONS: length 35 feet 4 inches (11.55 m); width 10 feet 8 inches (3.52 m); height 7 feet 5 inches (2.49 m)
RANGE: 250 miles (400 km)
ARMOR: classified
ARMAMENT: 1 x 120 mm gun; two 7.62 mm machine guns; 2 x smoke rocket dischargers
POWERPLANT: 1 x liquid-cooled diesel engine developing 1200 hp (895 kW)
PERFORMANCE: maximum road speed 35.6 mph (57 km/h); fording 3 feet 3 inches (1 m); vertical obstacle 2 feet 11 inches (0.9 m); trench 9 feet 2 inches (2.8 m)

ENGESA EE-9 Cascavel

The EE-9 was produced by the Brazilian armaments company ENGESA in the early 1970s as an attempt to replace obsolete US 6 x 6 M8 Greyhound armored cars. It is itself a 6 x 6 vehicle, which originally utilized the M8 turret on the Mk I Cascavel. Subsequent indigenous models featured an ENGESA turret with 90 mm gun, though the Mk II export model had the French Hispano-Suiza H-90 turret. Most modern Cascavels are fitted with computerized fire-control systems and laser range-finders. NBC protection is a further option. The Cascavel also has excellent lightweight armor developed by ENGESA and the University of São Paulo in a joint program.

SPECIFICATIONS

COUNTRY OF ORIGIN: Brazil
CREW: 3
WEIGHT: 29,500 pounds (13,400 kg)
DIMENSIONS: length (with gun) 20 feet 4 inches (6.2 m); width 8 feet 6 inches (2.59 m); height 8 feet 10 inches (2.6 m)
RANGE: 545 miles (880 km)
ARMOR: 0.62 inches (16 mm)
ARMAMENT: 1 x 90 mm cannon; 1 x coaxial MG, some versions 1 x 12.7 mm or 7.62 mm turret-mounted MG
POWERPLANT: 1 x Detroit Diesel 6V-53 6-cylinder diesel developing 212 hp (158 kW)
PERFORMANCE: maximum road speed 60 mph (100 km/h); fording 3 feet 4 inches (1 m); gradient 60 percent; vertical obstacle 2 feet (0.6 m)

ENGESA EE-T1 Osorio

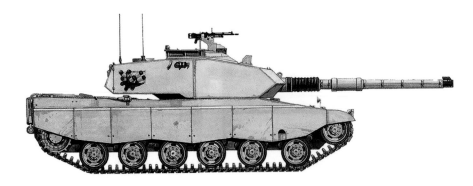

Designed to meet both home and export markets, the first prototype Osorio was completed in 1985. The layout is conventional with laser rangefinder, stabilizers to allow firing while on the move and thermal-imaging cameras, as well as a full nuclear, biological, and chemical (NBC) defense system. The tank can be fitted with two different sizes of main guns. Variants include a bridgelayer, armored recovery vehicle, and an anti-aircraft gun vehicle. There is little innovation in the design of the Osorio compared to the latest designs being produced in Europe and the United States. However, it is attractive for smaller countries that lack the capacity to manufacture their own main battle tank and for whom the European and American tanks are too expensive and complicated.

SPECIFICATIONS

COUNTRY OF ORIGIN: Brazil
CREW: 4
WEIGHT: 85,800 pounds (39,000 kg)
DIMENSIONS: length 32 feet 9 inches (9.99 m); width 10 feet 8 inches (3.26 m); height 7 feet 9 inches (2.37 m)
RANGE: 342 miles (550 km)
ARMOR: classified
ARMAMENT: 1 x British 105 mm/French 120 mm gun; 1 x 7.62 mm machine gun
POWERPLANT: 1 x 12-cylinder diesel engine developing 1000 hp (745 kW)
PERFORMANCE: maximum road speed 43.5 mph (70 km/h); fording 3 feet 11 inches (1.20 m); vertical obstacle 3 feet 4 inches (1.15 m); trench 9 feet 10 inches (3 m)

Guided Multiple Launch Rocket System (GMLRS)

Having initially been developed to improve the accuracy of the M26 rocket, the US military continues to refine the GMLRS, which is compatible with the existing M270 or HIMARS launchers. Potential vulnerability to a new generation of accurate long-range rocket and artillery ammunition prompted research on the GMLRS, which extends the range of the older M26 to 37.28 miles (60 km). The GMLRS currently includes two types of ammunition, the dual-purpose improved cluster munition (DPICM), which carries 404 bomblets, and the M31A1 rocket, with a single 200 pounds (91 kg) high-explosive warhead. Each is guided by a global positioning system with internal measurement unit guidance. The GMLRS provides greater range, more accurate fire, and therefore better results with fewer rockets. It also enhances the shoot-and-scoot capabilities of the HIMARS and M270 launchers, which have seen action in both Iraq and Afghanistan.

SPECIFICATIONS

COUNTRY OF ORIGIN: United States
CALIBRE: 127 mm
OPERATING SYSTEM: Inertial guidance with GPS
WEIGHT: 55,005 pounds (24,950 kg)
LENGTH: (overall) 22 feet 6 inches (6.86 m)
SHELL TYPE: 127 mm solid-fuel rocket with submunitions payload (M30 DPICM) or unitary (M31A1 Unitary) warhead
MAXIMUM ROCKET RANGE: 43.48 miles (70 km)
PERFORMANCE: road speed 40 mph (64 km/h); range 300 miles (483 km); engine type 500 hp (373 kW) Cummins diesel

K2 Black Panther MBT

The K2 Black Panther is one of the most expensive tanks in the world to date. Conceived as a replacement for the K1 MBT, using indigenous technology, it has been under development since 1995 and is expected to go into service in 2014. The Black Panther is protected by an advanced modular armor system, using easily replaced slabs of composite armor augmented by a countermeasures and active protection system. It is thought that the K2 has an equivalent level of protection to the M1 Abrams. The main gun is a 120 mm smoothbore weapon capable of delivering a range of munitions. These include conventional anti-tank ammunition and the Korean Smart Top-Attack Munition (KSTAM), which can be fired from a concealed position to engage enemy armor at a range of up to 4.97 miles (8 km). There are plans to export the K2, with Turkey as one of the first customers.

SPECIFICATIONS

COUNTRY OF ORIGIN: South Korea
CREW: 3
WEIGHT: 121,254 pounds (55 tonnes)
DIMENSIONS: length 24 feet 7 inches (7.5 m); width 11 feet 9 inches (3.6 m); height 8 feet 2 inches (2.5 m)
RANGE: 267 miles (430 km)
ARMOR: classified, advanced composite
ARMAMENT: 1 x 120 mm smoothbore cannon; 1 x 12.7 mm machine gun; 1 x 7.62 mm machine gun
POWERPLANT: MTU MB-883 Ka500 diesel
PERFORMANCE: maximum road speed 43 mph (70 km/h)

KIFV K-200

The Korean Infantry Fighting Vehicle K-200 is the first of a series of South Korean fighting vehicles developed by the Dae Woo Industries company. Borrowing from the US AIFV, it has become a powerful and reliable armored personnel carrier. It can carry nine infantry and its three-man crew into battle at speeds of 46 mph (74 km/h). In amphibious mode, it achieves 4 mph (7 km/h) on water, propelled by its tracks. Standard armament is usually two machine guns a 12.7 mm and a 7.62 mm weapon. However, optional armament configurations include 20 mm Vulcan cannon and two mortar carriers: 8 mm and 106 m. An NBC reconnaissance variant has recently been developed.

SPECIFICATIONS

COUNTRY OF ORIGIN: South Korea
CREW: 3 + 9
WEIGHT: 28,400 pounds (12,900 kg)
DIMENSIONS: length 18 feet (5.48 m); width 9 feet 4 inches (2.84 m); height 8 feet 3 inches (2.51 m)
RANGE: 300 miles (480 km)
ARMOR: aluminium and steel (details classified)
ARMAMENT: 1 x 12.7 mm MG; 1 x 7.62 mm machine gun
POWERPLANT: 1 x MAN D-284T V8 diesel, developing 280 hp (208 kW) at 2300rpm
PERFORMANCE: maximum road speed 46 mph (74 km/h); fording amphibious; gradient 60 percent; vertical obstacle 2 feet 1 inches (0.64 m); trench: 5 feet 6 inches (1.68 m)

Leclerc

The Leclerc was designed to replace the French Army's fleet of AMX-30 tanks. Development began in 1983 and the first production Leclercs appeared in 1991. The Leclerc is an excellent vehicle. An automatic loading system for the main armament and remote-control machine guns allow the crew to be cut down to three. The tank can be fitted with extra fuel tanks to increase operational range and standard equipment includes a fire-detection/suppression system, thermal-imaging and laser rangefinder for the main gun, plus a land navigation system. The on-board electronic systems are fully integrated to allow automatic reconfiguration in case of battlefield failure or damage. As well as in French service, around 390 Leclercs have been exported to the United Arab Emirates.

SPECIFICATIONS

COUNTRY OF ORIGIN: France
CREW: 3
WEIGHT: 117,700 pounds (53,500 kg)
DIMENSIONS: length 32 feet 5 inches (9.87 m); width 11 feet 4 inches (3.71 m); height 7 feet 6 inches (2.46 m)
RANGE: 345 miles (550 km)
ARMOR: classified
ARMAMENT: 1 x 120 mm gun, one 12.7 mm machine gun, one 7.62 mm MG, 3 x 9 smoke dischargers
POWERPLANT: 1 x SAEM UDU V8X 1500 T9 Hyperbar eight-cylinder diesel engine developing 1500 hp (1119 kW); SESM ESM500 automatic transmission
PERFORMANCE: maximum road speed 45.6 mph (73 km/h); fording 3 feet 3 inches (1 m); vertical obstacle 4 feet 1 inches (1.25 m); trench 9 feet 10 inches (3 m)

M1 Abrams

The M1 Abrams was the next stage in American tank development after the M60. Chrysler completed the prototypes in 1978 and the first production vehicles appeared in 1980, with 30 tanks a month being built in following years. Its advanced Chobham armor makes the M1 the best protected US main battle tank yet. Its gas turbine engine is smaller and easier to service than a diesel engine, but the extra fuel requirement negates the space saved, which is perhaps why the idea was rejected for the Leopard 2. Thermal sights, laser rangefinder, and gun stabilization system give the M1 excellent firepower on the move, be it day or night. In the 1991 Gulf War, the Abrams proved itself the best tank in the world, knocking out Iraqi T72s with impunity with no Abrams destroyed by enemy fire.

SPECIFICATIONS

COUNTRY OF ORIGIN: United States
CREW: 4
WEIGHT: 119,392 pounds (54,269 kg)
DIMENSIONS: length 32 feet (9.76 m); width 12 feet (3.65 m); height 9 feet 6 inches (2.89 m)
RANGE: 280 miles (450 km)
ARMOR: classified
ARMAMENT: 1 x 105 mm gun; two 7.62 mm machine guns (one coaxial, one on loader's hatch); one 12.7 mm machine gun
POWERPLANT: Avco Lycoming AGT-1500 gas turbine, developing 1500 hp (1119 kW)
PERFORMANCE: maximum road speed 45 mph (72.5k m/h); fording 4 feet (1.22 m); vertical obstacle 4 feet 1 inches (1.24 m); trench 9 feet (2.74 m)

M2 Bradley

The M2 Bradley was the US Army's first mechanized infantry combat vehicle. The first production models appeared in 1981 and they were soon being produced at the rate of 600 per year. The hull of the M2 is made of aluminium, with a layer of spaced laminate armor for added protection. The 25 mm cannon has a stabilizer to allow for firing on the move. The troop compartment in the rear is fitted with firing ports and periscopes to allow the troops to fire from within the vehicle. Night vision and a nuclear, biological, and chemical (NBC) defense system are standard. The Bradley plays a key role in the US Army's combined arms concept, but critics say it is too big, too expensive, and too difficult to maintain. It is also insufficiently armored to operate with main battle tanks on the battlefield.

SPECIFICATIONS

COUNTRY OF ORIGIN: United States
CREW: 3 + 7
WEIGHT: 22,666 kg (49,865 pounds)
DIMENSIONS: length 21 feet 2 inches (6.453 m); width 10 feet 6 inches (3.2 m); height; 9 feet 10 inches (2.97 m)
RANGE: 300 miles (483 km)
ARMOR: classified
ARMAMENT: 1 x Hughes Helicopter 25 mm Chain Gun; 1 x 7.62 mm coaxial machine gun; 2 x anti-tank launchers.
POWERPLANT: 1 x Cummins 8-cylinder diesel, developing 500 hp (373 kW)
PERFORMANCE: maximum road speed 41 mph (66 km/h); fording amphibious; vertical obstacle 3 feet (0.91 m); trench 8 feet 4 inches (2.54 m)

M35

Developed after World War II, the M35, known as the "Eager Beaver", became the standard US Army 6 x 6 truck and was the most widely used military truck in the West, with the US Army alone having 65,000 in use. By early 1980, AM General had produced over 150,000 M35/44 series 6 x 6 trucks. Initially equipped with a gas engine, later versions were converted to multi-fuel and diesel systems to make them more fuel-efficient. Other improvements included a redesigned suspension, brakes and steering, plus a forward-tilting hood. Optional extras were a winch, special heating for cold-weather operations, deep-fording equipment, and center troop seats for carrying personnel. The many variations of the M35 included the M48 tractor truck, M50 water tanker, M59 Dumper, M60 wrecker, and M185 repair van.

SPECIFICATIONS

COUNTRY OF ORIGIN: United States
CREW: 1 + 2
WEIGHT: 17,969 pounds (8168 kg)
DIMENSIONS: length 22 feet (6.71 m); width 7 feet 10 inches (2.39 m); height 9 feet 6 inches (2.9 m)
RANGE: 300 miles (483 km)
ARMOR: none
ARMAMENT: none
POWERPLANT: 1 x LDT-465-IC 6-cylinder diesel engine developing 140 hp (104 kW)
PERFORMANCE: maximum road speed 56 mph (90 km/h); fording 2 feet 6 inches (0.76 m)

M998

The High Mobility Multi-Purpose Wheeled Vehicle (HMMWV) — "Hummer" — prototype appeared in August 1980 and in March 1983, AM General was awarded a contract to build 54,973 vehicles, of which 39,000 were for the US Army. The vehicle has a four-man crew, who sit on either side of the drive chain, which allows for a low center of gravity. The frame is strong enough to serve as a roll bar and support for various equipment kits. The Hummer can also mount a variety of weapons, such as the TOW anti-tank system, 7.62 mm and 12.7 mm machine guns, Mk 19 40 mm grenade launchers, and even batteries of Stinger surface-to-air missiles (SAMs). The vehicle has a fully synchronized transmission with 16 forward and eight reverse gears. The M998 has been exported to the Middle East and Asia.

SPECIFICATIONS

COUNTRY OF ORIGIN: United States
CREW: 1 + 3
WEIGHT: 8375 pounds (3870 kg)
DIMENSIONS: length 14 feet 8 inches (4.46 m); width 7 feet (2.15 m); height 5 feet 8 inches (1.75 m)
RANGE: 352 miles (563 km)
ARMOR: not applicable
ARMAMENT: various, including machine guns, grenade launchers and surface-to-air missile (SAM) launchers
POWERPLANT: 1 x V-8 6.21 air-cooled diesel engine developing 135 hp (101 kW)
PERFORMANCE: maximum road range 65.6 mph (105 km/h); fording 2 feet 6 inches (0.76 m); vertical obstacle 1 feet 9 inches (0.56 m)

Merkava

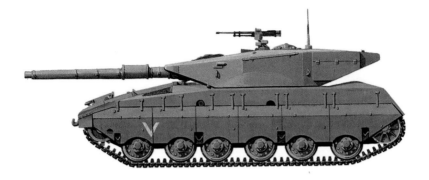

Prior to the Six-Day War in 1967, Israel had relied on Sherman and Centurion tanks for its armored forces. However, doubts about future supplies and also concerns that these tanks did not fully meet Israeli requirements prompted development of an indigenous tank. The first Merkavas appeared in 1980 and saw action for the first time against Syrian forces in Lebanon in 1982. Compared to other modern main battle tanks, the Merkava is slow and has a poor power-to-weight ratio. However, it is designed for specific tactical requirements, which differ from those of most other tank producers. The emphasis is on crew survivability, which explains the Merkava's small cross-section that makes it less of a target and the well-sloped armor for greatest protection.

SPECIFICATIONS

COUNTRY OF ORIGIN: Israel
CREW: 4
WEIGHT: 122,976 (55,898 kg pounds)
DIMENSIONS: length 27 feet 5 inches (8.36 m); width 12 feet 3 inches (3.72 m); height 8 feet 8 inches (2.64 m)
RANGE: 310 miles (500 km)
ARMOR: classified
ARMAMENT: 1 x 105 mm rifled gun; one 7.62 mm machine gun
POWERPLANT: 1 x Teledyne Continental AVDS-1790-6A V-12 diesel engine developing 900 hp (671 kW)
PERFORMANCE: maximum road speed 28.6 mph (46 km/h); vertical obstacle 3 feet 3 inches (1 m); trench 9 feet 10 inches (3 m)

MLRS

The Vought Multiple Launch Rocket System (MLRS) is among the most powerful land weapons of NATO forces today. Using the chassis of the M2 Infantry Fighting Vehicle, Vought created a Self-Propelled Launcher Loader (SPLL) vehicle, which mounted 12 M26 unguided free-flight rockets in two six-missile pods (together known as the M270 launcher unit). Each standard rocket contains 644 M77 submunitions that scatter widely over the area of impact. Consequently, each M26 is able to assault an area of 0.09miles^2 (0.23km^2). During the Gulf War, Iraqi units nicknamed the MLRS "steel rain" on account of its accurate and relentless attacks. Other warheads include biological or chemical munitions and anti-tank mines.

SPECIFICATIONS

COUNTRY OF ORIGIN: United States
CREW: 3
WEIGHT: 55,546 pounds (25,191 kg)
DIMENSIONS: length 22 feet 4 inches (6.8 m); width 9 feet 7 inches (2.92 m); height 8 feet 6 inches (2.6 m)
RANGE: 300 miles (480 km)
ARMOR: details classified
ARMAMENT: 12 x MLRS rockets
POWERPLANT: 1 x Cummins VTA-903 8-cylinder turbo diesel, developing 500 hp (373 kW)
PERFORMANCE: maximum road speed 40mph (64 km/h); fording 3 feet 7 inches (1.1 m); gradient 60 percent; vertical obstacle 3 feet 3 inches (1 m)

Pinzgauer Vector PPV 6 x 6

The Pinzgauer family of 4 x 4 and 6 x 6 vehicles was originally developed in Austria and has been supplied to military users worldwide as a tactical and utility vehicle and as a light artillery tractor. An ambulance version is also available and the vehicle family has found favor on the civilian market for use as a rescue and exploration vehicle, or as a fire engine. The 6 x 6 Vector is manufactured in the UK and serves as a patrol and command vehicle. It carries no armament as standard but can be fitted with one or two 7.62 mm machine guns when necessary. The Vector was introduced in 2007 in an effort to provide troops serving in Afghanistan with better-protected patrol vehicles. While it proved to possess extremely good off road capability, the Vector was not a success as it lacked mine and improvised explosive device (IED) protection.

SPECIFICATIONS

COUNTRY OF ORIGIN: United Kingdom
CREW: 2 + 4 additional personnel
WEIGHT: 14,550 pounds (6600 kg)
DIMENSIONS: length 17 feet 5 inches (5.3 m); width 5 feet 11 inches (1.8 m); height 6 feet 11 inches (2.1 m)
RANGE: 248 miles (400 km)
ARMOR: classified
ARMAMENT: up to 2 x 7.62 mm machine guns
POWERPLANT: WW 5-cylinder Euro 3
PERFORMANCE: maximum road speed 62 mph (100 km/h)

RBY Mk 1

The RBY Mk 1 is a light reconnaissance vehicle first manufactured by Israel Aircraft Industries in the mid-1970s. Though the hull is all-welded steel with 0.31 inches (8 mm) armor, there is no top cover for the crew compartment. Also, the front windscreen can be folded flat for unimpaired visibility. These features increase the RBY's vulnerability to small arms and shell fire, but reduce the chances of occupant heat exhaustion in the hot Middle Eastern climate. A variety of machine guns and cannon, even a 106 mm recoilless rifle, can be fitted to the rim of the hull. The RBY Mk 1's hood and bumpers are made of fiberglass designed to disintegrate harmlessly if the vehicle strikes a mine.

SPECIFICATIONS

COUNTRY OF ORIGIN: Israel
CREW: 2 + 6
WEIGHT: 7900 pounds (3600 kg)
DIMENSIONS: length 16 feet 6 inches (5.02 m); width 6 feet 8 inches (2.03 m); height 5 feet 5 inches (1.66 m)
RANGE: 340 miles (550 km)
ARMOR: (steel) 0.31 inches (8 mm)
ARMAMENT: various machine gun and cannons
POWERPLANT: 1 x Chrysler 6-cylinder petrol, developing 120 hp (89 kW)
PERFORMANCE: maximum road speed 62 mph (100 km/h); fording 1 feet 4 inches (0.4 m); gradient 60 percent

Rooikat

The Rooikat is one of the world's most potent armored cars. Its development program began in 1978, but it took 12 years before it was ready to enter service in 1990. Two main versions are available. The Rooikat 76 has a stabilized 76 mm gun and the Rooikat 105 has an even more powerful 105 mm anti-tank gun, which can fire six rounds per minute. Such firepower allows the Rooikat to make aggressive seek-and-destroy missions as well as combat reconnaissance. The classified armored type protects the crew from anti-tank mines and small arms ammunition up to 24 mm caliber. All tires have run-flat inserts; mobility is maintained even with loss of pressure in all eight tires.

SPECIFICATIONS

COUNTRY OF ORIGIN: South Africa
CREW: 4
WEIGHT: 61,700 pounds (28,000 kg)
DIMENSIONS: length 23 feet 3 inches (7.09 m); width 9 feet 6 inches (2.9 m); height 9 feet 2 inches (2.8 m)
RANGE: 620 miles (1000 km)
ARMOR: classified
ARMAMENT: 1 x 76 mm gun (Rooikat 76); 1 x 105 mm gun (Rooikat 105); 1 x coaxial 7.62 mm machine gun; 1 x turret-mounted 7.62 mm machine gun; 2 x 4 smoke grenade launchers
POWERPLANT: 1 x V-10 diesel, developing 563 hp (420 kW)
PERFORMANCE: maximum road speed 75 mph (120 km/h); fording 4 feet 11 inches (1.5 m); gradient 70 percent; vertical obstacle 3 feet 3 inches (1 m); trench 6 feet 7 inches (2 m)

SAS Land Rover

The British Special Air Service (SAS) has made good use of a long-wheelbase version of the Land Rover, specially adapted for the conditions faced in the types of low-intensity warfare in which the SAS has become expert. Painted pink for camouflage during desert operations (where its color blends in with the desert haze) and known as Pink Panthers, the vehicles used a similar chassis to that of ordinary British Army Land Rovers. Widely used in the Persian Gulf, they were equipped with metal sand-crossing channels, smoke dischargers, and machine guns. In addition, they carried specialist navigational equipment and external stowage racks, to give them the capability to carry out long-range desert reconnaissance missions behind enemy lines.

SPECIFICATIONS

COUNTRY OF ORIGIN: United Kingdom
CREW: 1
WEIGHT: 6710 pounds (3050 kg)
DIMENSIONS: length 15 feet 4 inches (4.67 m); width 5 feet 11 inches (1.79 m); height 6 feet 8 inches (2.03 m)
RANGE: 4655 miles (748 km)
ARMAMENT: 2 x 7.62 mm machine guns
POWERPLANT: 1 x V-8 water-cooled petrol engine developing 134 hp (100 kW)
PERFORMANCE: maximum road speed 65.6 mph (105 km/h); fording 1 feet 7 inches (0.5 m)

Spähpanzer 2 Luchs

Having previously relied on American or European imports, West Germany began to develop a range of indigenous armored vehicles during the 1960s. In 1975, Thyssen Henschel began production of an 8 x 8 armored reconnaissance vehicle — the Luchs — completing 408 before 1978. Too expensive for significant export success, the vehicle was well-armored and came with a range of extras such as power steering to reduce driver fatigue, night vision, a nuclear, biological, and chemical (NBC) system, and pre-heating for the engine, essential for winter operations. Fully amphibious, the vehicle has an exceptional operational range. In the water it is powered by two propellers mounted at the rear of the vehicle. The turret has full power traverse through 360 degrees.

SPECIFICATIONS

COUNTRY OF ORIGIN: West Germany
CREW: 4
WEIGHT: 42,900 pounds (19,500 kg)
DIMENSIONS: length 25 feet 5 inches (7.74 m); width 9 feet 9 inches (2.98 m); height (including anti-aircraft machine gun) 9 feet 6 inches (2.91 m)
RANGE: 500 miles (800 km)
ARMOR: classified
ARMAMENT: 1 x 20 mm cannon; one 7.62 mm machine gun
POWERPLANT: 1 x Daimler-Benz OM 403 A 10-cylinder diesel engine developing 390 hp (291 kW)
PERFORMANCE: maximum road speed 56 mph (90 km/h); fording amphibious; vertical obstacle 2 feet (0.6 m); trench 6 feet 3 inches (1.9 m)

Stingray

The prototype of the Stingray was unveiled in 1984 by Cadillac Gage, who had foreseen the need for a light tank with good mobility and firepower, which was simple to operate and maintain. Wherever possible, proven parts from other vehicles have been adapted to save development costs. The Stingray comes equipped with laser rangefinder, stabilization devices for the gun, nuclear, biological, and chemical (NBC) protection, and has the firepower of a main battle tank. Its drawback is its light armor. However, given the power of modern high explosive anti-tank (HEAT) rounds, this may make little difference. The Stingray has performance and power at a much lower unit cost when compared to a main battle tank and is thus the subject of great interest around the world.

SPECIFICATIONS

COUNTRY OF ORIGIN: United States
CREW: 4
WEIGHT: 41,912 pounds (19,051 kg)
DIMENSIONS: length 30 feet 8 inches (9.35 m); width 8 feet 11 inches (2.71 m); height 8 feet 4 inches (2.54 m)
RANGE: 300 miles (483 km)
ARMOR: classified
ARMAMENT: 1 x 105 mm rifled gun; one coaxial 7.62 mm machine gun; one 7.62 mm anti-aircraft machine gun
POWERPLANT: 1 x Diesel Model 8V-92 TA diesel engine developing 399 kW (535 hp)
PERFORMANCE: maximum road speed 43 mph (69 km/h); fording 4 feet (1.22 m); vertical obstacle 2 feet 6 inches (0.76 m); trench 5 feet 7 inches (1.69 m)

Stryker ICV

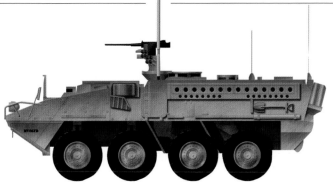

The eight-wheeled Stryker armored fighting vehicle entered service with the US Army in 2002. Its mobility and protection have been instrumental during operations in Iraq. Its weapons systems are remotely controlled from inside the vehicle. The basic Stryker is a fast, advanced armored personnel carrier capable of carrying nine troops and supporting them in action. It is protected against rockets and machine-gun fire; additional armor can be applied when necessary. Several versions are available including command, engineering support, mortar carrier, and anti-tank missile versions, plus a Mobile Gun System armed with a 105 mm gun. This is too lightly protected to serve as a replacement for main battle tanks, but offers direct fire support to a Stryker-mobile force. One advantage of using the same vehicle for many roles is ease of maintenance and improved availability of replacement vehicles.

SPECIFICATIONS

COUNTRY OF ORIGIN: United States
CREW: 2 + 9
WEIGHT: 36,234 pounds (16,470 kg)
DIMENSIONS: length 22 feet 10 inches (6.95 m); width 8 feet 11 inches (2.72 m); height 2.64 m (8 feet 8 inches)
RANGE: 310 miles (500 km)
ARMOR: Stryker reactive armor tiles (SRAT) for protection against rocket attack
ARMAMENT: M2 12.7 mm machine gun or Mk 19 40 mm grenade launcher mounted in a PROTECTOR M151 Remote Weapon Station (RWS) (ICV)
POWERPLANT: 350 hp (260 kW) Caterpillar C7 diesel
PERFORMANCE: speed 62 mph (100 km/h)

TAM

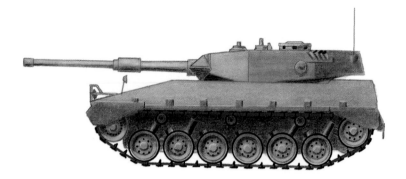

For many years, the Argentinian Army relied on World War II Sherman tanks to form the basis of its armored forces. By the early 1970s, these were becoming difficult to maintain. Most foreign tanks of the period were too heavy for domestic conditions and thus a new tank was ordered from Thyssen Henschel of West Germany. Once developed, production moved to Buenos Aires and production began towards the end of the 1970s. The hull of the TAM was based on that of the MICV in use with the West German Army. The armor is comparatively poor against that of other main battle tanks, such as the Leopard 1 and the AMX-30, but is well-sloped to give as much protection as possible. The tank was not produced in time to have any impact on the 1982 Falklands conflict.

SPECIFICATIONS

COUNTRY OF ORIGIN: Argentina
CREW: 4
WEIGHT: 67,100 pounds (30,500 kg)
DIMENSIONS: length (gun forward) 25 feet 2 inches (8.23 m); width 9 feet 6 inches (3.12 m); height 7 feet 5 inches (2.42 m)
RANGE: 560 miles (900 km)
ARMOR: classified
ARMAMENT: 1 x 105 mm gun; one coaxial 7.62 mm machine gun; one 7.62 mm anti-aircraft machine gun
POWERPLANT: one V-6 turbo-charged diesel engine developing 720 hp (537 kW)
PERFORMANCE: maximum road speed 46.9 mph (75 km/h); fording 4 feet 11 inches (1.5 m); vertical obstacle 3 feet 3 inches (1 m); trench 8 feet 2 inches (2.5 m)

Type 69

The Type 69 was the replacement for the Type 59. First seen in public in 1982, during a parade in Beijing, the tank was very similar in appearance to the Type 59, but was fitted with a new 105/106 mm gun, probably based on that of the Soviet T-62, examples of which were captured by the Chinese during border clashes with the Soviet Union. There are a number of versions, including a self-propelled anti-aircraft gun, armored bridgelayer, and armored recovery vehicle. The latter has a Type 69 chassis, but the turret removed and replaced by a superstructure; there is also a dozer blade at the front and crane at the rear. Large quantities of the Type 69 were exported to Iraq in the early 1980s, with Saudi Arabia acting as intermediary, to make up for losses experienced during the war with Iraq.

SPECIFICATIONS

COUNTRY OF ORIGIN: China
CREW: 4
WEIGHT: 80,300 pounds (36,500 kg)
DIMENSIONS: length 26 feet 6 inches (8.68 m); width (3.3 m); height 8 feet 10 inches (2.87 m)
RANGE: 250 miles (375 km)
ARMOR: 3.94 inches (100 mm)
ARMAMENT: 1 x 100 mm gun; one 12.7 mm machine gun; two 7.62 mm machine guns; 2 x smoke rocket dischargers
POWERPLANT: 1 x V-12 liquid-cooled diesel engine developing 580 hp (432 kW)
PERFORMANCE: maximum road speed 31.3 mph (50 km/h); fording 4 feet 7 inches (1.4 m); vertical obstacle 2 feet 7 inches (0.8 m); trench 8 feet 10 inches (2.7 m)

Warrior

The Warrior Mechanized Combat Vehicle entered development in 1972 and entered service with the British Army in 1987. The Warrior was part of a movement to change armored personnel carriers from their role of merely transporting troops to and from the battlefield into a more capable infantry combat vehicle, this concept being inspired by the success of the Soviet BMP. Designed to supplement the FV432, the Warrior is heavier and much more heavily armored. It is treated as a mobile fire base from which troops can fight, rather than a mere transport vehicle. Versions include a command vehicle, recovery vehicle, engineer, and observation vehicle. It has been sold to Kuwait, whose Warriors have anti-tank launchers each side of the turret and air conditioning.

SPECIFICATIONS

COUNTRY OF ORIGIN: United Kingdom
CREW: 3 + 7
WEIGHT: 56,540 pounds (25,700 kg)
DIMENSIONS: length 20 feet 10 inches (6.34 m); width 10 feet (3.03 m); height 9 feet 2 inches (2.79 m)
RANGE: 412 miles (660 km)
ARMOR: classified
ARMAMENT: 1 x 30 mm Rarden cannon; 1 x 7.62 mm co-axial machine gun; 4 x smoke dischargers
POWERPLANT: 1 x Perkins V-8 diesel engine developing 550 hp (410 kW)
PERFORMANCE: maximum road speed 46.8 mph (75 km/h); fording 4 feet 3 inches (1.3 m); vertical obstacle 2 feet 5 inches (0.75 m); trench 8 feet 2 inches (2.5 m)

Zulfiqar Main Battle Tank

The Zulfiqar MBT seems to be a composite design constructed from components for T72s and systems either developed indigenously or copied from existing tank designs. The latter may include the M48 and M60. Three versions have been observed, though the Zulfiqar 2 was apparently an interim vehicle serving as a test bed for the Zulfigar 3 design. The latter bears some resemblance to the US M-1 Abrams, though it is less technologically sophisticated. Armor is of steel for the most part, with composite armor used in the frontal arc. Reactive armor may also be available. The Zulfiqar 3 is armed with a 125 mm smoothbore gun which is probably fed by an autoloader and aimed by a ballistic computer. It is thought that the tank has a crew of three and may be fitted with an NBC protection system.

SPECIFICATIONS

COUNTRY OF ORIGIN: Iran
CREW: 3 or 4
WEIGHT: probably around 88,185 pounds (40,000 kg)
DIMENSIONS: length approx. 23 feet (7 m); width approx. 11 feet 9 inches (3.6 m); height approx. 8 feet 2 inches (2.5 m)
RANGE: possibly around 311 miles (500 km)
ARMOR: unknown
ARMAMENT: 1 x 125 mm smoothbore gun, 1 x 12.7 mm machine gun; 1 x 7.62 mm machine gun
POWERPLANT: diesel of unknown type
PERFORMANCE: possibly 37–43mph (60–70 km/h)

MILITARY VEHICLES 1980 TO TODAY

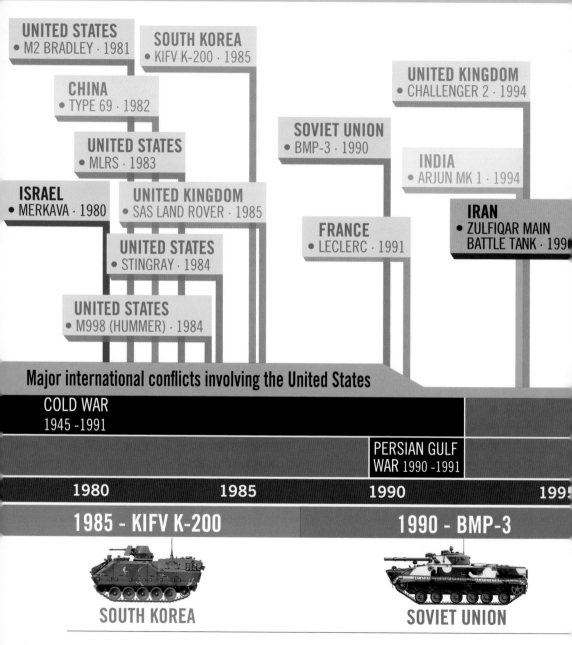

UNITED STATES
- M2 BRADLEY · 1981

SOUTH KOREA
- KIFV K-200 · 1985

CHINA
- TYPE 69 · 1982

UNITED STATES
- MLRS · 1983

ISRAEL
- MERKAVA · 1980

UNITED KINGDOM
- SAS LAND ROVER · 1985

UNITED STATES
- STINGRAY · 1984

UNITED STATES
- M998 (HUMMER) · 1984

UNITED KINGDOM
- CHALLENGER 2 · 1994

SOVIET UNION
- BMP-3 · 1990

INDIA
- ARJUN MK 1 · 1994

FRANCE
- LECLERC · 1991

IRAN
- ZULFIQAR MAIN BATTLE TANK · 1996

Major international conflicts involving the United States

COLD WAR
1945 -1991

PERSIAN GULF WAR 1990 -1991

| 1980 | 1985 | 1990 | 1995 |

1985 - KIFV K-200

1990 - BMP-3

SOUTH KOREA

SOVIET UNION

FEATURED WEAPONS TIMELINE

This timeline features notable advancements in military technologies by influential nations worldwide.

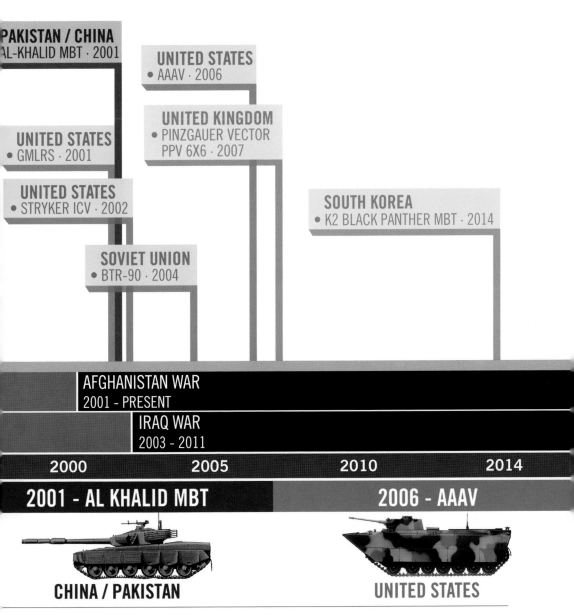

PAKISTAN / CHINA
AL-KHALID MBT · 2001

UNITED STATES
• AAAV · 2006

UNITED KINGDOM
• PINZGAUER VECTOR PPV 6X6 · 2007

UNITED STATES
• GMLRS · 2001

UNITED STATES
• STRYKER ICV · 2002

SOUTH KOREA
• K2 BLACK PANTHER MBT · 2014

SOVIET UNION
• BTR-90 · 2004

AFGHANISTAN WAR
2001 - PRESENT

IRAQ WAR
2003 - 2011

| 2000 | 2005 | 2010 | 2014 |

2001 - AL KHALID MBT

2006 - AAAV

CHINA / PAKISTAN

UNITED STATES

Glossary

amphibious vessels
can be used on land and in water

armament
a nation's strength of military weapons used in a war

depleted uranium
contains less of the isotope uranium-235 that is found in the natural form of uranium and is used in anti-tank weapons and other armaments

deployment
to be utilized as in military personnel or equipment

fin-stabilized
a device on the vertical tail structure to steady an aircraft

guerilla forces
an armed force, usually in large groups and rural areas, that fights by sabotage and harassment

infrared rays
light rays that can appear as a black and grey image on a display device

land mine
an explosive charge concealed under the surface of the ground that is detonated by the pressure of a vehicle or person

logistics
managing and organizing the details of an operation

maligned
harmful untruths

materiel
equipment and supplies used by soldiers

NERA (non-energetic reactive armor)
a form of armor that can withstand multiple hits; but a second hit in the same location will penetrate the armor

reactive armor
a type of vehicle armor that reacts to the impact of a weapon and reduces the damage to the vehicle

reconnaissance
the inspection or exploration of an area to gather military information

smoothbore cannon
projectiles in cannons with smooth barrels have no significant spin when they are fired and can be less accurate

strategists
person who is skilled in forming strategies and making plans for achieving a goal

tactician
person who is skilled in the planning and execution of military tactics in combat

turrets
a revolving domelike structure on a military tank, plane, or ship with guns mounted on it

Further Information

Websites

http://www.militaryfactory.com/armor/index.asp
Military tanks, carrier, and anti-tank vehicles are presented by decade.

http://www.transchool.lee.army.mil/museum/transportation%20museum/desertstorm.htm
The US Army Transportation Museum covers military transportation from colonial days to the present, including Desert Storm and Afghanistan.

www.mvpa.org/
The Military Vehicle Preservation Association is an international organization dedicated to the collection and restoration of historic military vehicles.

www.mvtf.org/
See one of the largest collections of historical military vehicles, overseen by the Military Vehicle Technology Foundation.

Books

Bradford, George. *World War II AFV Plans: American Armored Fighting Vehicles.* Stackpole Books, 2007.
View technical drawings of the military vehicles used in WWII, produced by an artist and military historian.

Dell, Pamela. *The Science of Military Vehicles.* Capstone Press, 2012.
Discusses how science and technology has changed military vehicles through the years.

Neville, Leigh and Richard Chasemore. *Special Operations Patrol Vehicles: Afghanistan and Iraq.* Osprey Publishing, 2011.
This book includes tactical and non-standard tactical vehicles.

Ware, Pat. *A Complete Directory of Military Vehicles.* Anness Publishing, 2012.
The book features images and text for more than 180 military vehicles.

Index of Military Vehicles Profile Pages